PHOTO WALK LOG

Published by EnergyBook - RW Jemmett

First Edition

© RW Jemmett 2022

ISBN 978-1-8383047-5-1

ABOUT THIS LOG BOOK

This Photo Walk Log book has been designed to help you enjoy and get the most from your Photo Walks.

The Log Book will help you whether you walk with a phone, film or digital camera. It can be used in all settings, from hiking in open rugged landscapes, to urban walks and street life adventures.

Resources to support this Photo Walk Log Book can be found at:

rwjemmett.com/photowalklog

PHOTO WALK TIPS

One - Enjoy your Photo Walk. Walking with a camera can be very enjoyable and you get the chance to take time to see and hear everything around you. Without a defined destination and timetable, it's great just to look, hear and capture. Try not to worry too much about whether you are capturing great images and think more about what you are seeing. There is a perhaps a difference between seeing and observing, just as there is a difference between hearing and listening. Be ready to take a photograph. Depending on the camera, I remove any lens cap for the whole walk and rely on a clear filter to cover and protect the lens. I also make sure I can quickly take my camera from any bag and sometimes use a wrist strap for ease.

Two - Check out your local area. You can, of course, travel with your camera but there are often great places to Photo Walk right on your doorstep. The local town centre and high street, parks, public footpaths, etc. Whether you like capturing people, nature, architecture, urban life, the weather, clues to the past, or a moment in time - you can usually do this in your local neighbourhood.

Three - Research before you Photo Walk. There are lots of tools for researching the area for your next Photo Walk. Depending on what you hope to capture you can look at maps (past and present), wikipedia, local history society websites, history books, guides to local arts, etc. Check for local market days and what flora and crops might be in flower. Anticipate what you may see - but also enjoy what you do see.

Four - Capture some information about your Photo Walk. Use this Log Book to capture some information about the walk. Think about what you may want to review when you process your images, when you plan your next Photo Walk and when you look back in a year or two.

Five - Safety and the law. Stay safe when you are out and about. It's easy to get caught up in the shoot and forget about where you are. Looking at the camera screen or through the viewfinder can make you a little vulnerable to hazards. You and your camera equipment need to be looked after. Safety hazards can include traffic (whether in a busy urban environment or a country lane), farm animals (especially cows) and people (people walking & jogging for example, may expect you to move as they approach in busy areas). Your equipment will also be attractive to some, so keep it safe and out of sight when not in use. To help, I like to carry my camera in a bag that does not look like a camera bag. Especially if I am carrying a larger camera. Also, I would advise not to use a neck strap where the camera hangs down in front of you. You should aim to blend in not stand out.

Please see this Log Book's Appendices for information about **The Law and Photography**

Six - Know your camera. The best way to get to know your camera is to use it - but it can be disappointing if your Photo Walk results are less than expected due to the wrong settings or camera handling. With a digital camera it is easy to practice using the controls and checking the results. With a film camera running a film through can be a little expensive so it is best to try out all the camera features before inserting a film. Try everything. Run through the menu, read the manual, watch a few YouTube videos, etc.

Seven - Keep it simple A Photo walk is often about opportunity rather than having lots of gear and spending a lot of time changing settings and lenses. With regards to settings, decide how you want to shoot (auto is OK). You may want to set your camera to get the best possible chance of a good image. An aperture of F8 to keep more of the scene in focus and a speed of around 1/125 to help prevent camera shake if you need to.

I try to minimise the amount of gear I carry. One camera and one lens. Zoom lenses are great if your camera will take one, but using a standard lens can make things simple and also allow you to think more about the shot. When post processing your shots, with Adobe Lightroom, for example, you can crop the image and therefore zoom in (but you cannot zoom out of course).

Hopefully, you will have remembered to charge the batteries or have new batteries available along with a spare SD card or film, lens cloth, etc. There is a handy equipment check at the end of this Log Book.

Eight - Mix it up and look for a story and a feeling. I like the images I shoot on my Photo Walk to capture my thoughts at the time and help communicate a feeling or story about the scene. The story and feelings can be found in the largest building, the dingiest alleyway, a passing glance, a magnificent tree or a small flower. It's up to you. Shoot what you like. Try to leave behind any thoughts about what a Photo Walk should be and photograph what you want, from a family member to a wide open landscape; from cracked paving to the hustle and bustle of a transport hub.

Nine - Set a theme. In contrast to 'mixing things up'. You may want to set yourself a theme for your images. Whether it is a wider theme such as people commuting, urban night photography, or wide open landscapes or a more specific theme like hidden nature, unused spaces, signs, doors, fences, insects, local history, a colour, architecture style, etc. Setting a theme can sometimes help you see more and help focus your creativity.

Ten - Focus on what you have with you. There is an old saying that 'the best camera is the one that you have with you.' Think about the gear you have with you and how you want to use it, whether it be a camera phone or an expensive DSLR with multiple lenses. Use your creativity to get great shots rather than just exploiting the features in your camera. If your camera has face recognition use it, but if not, don't spend the Photo Walk wishing it had. When you look at an impressive photograph taken by another photographer, I doubt you will say it was a shame that they did not have a camera with more megapixels. Enjoy using what you have and revel in the limitations. Shooting images with a simple film compact camera with fixed aperture and speed can give you great results - enjoy the images for what they are, not what they could be. A great photo does not have to be pixel perfect. Indeed, when you review the results of your Photo Walk, don't delete an image until you looked at it carefully think what is right and wrong about the image. And again how you feel about what you are viewing.

Eleven - Use post production techniques. Whether you use an App in your phone or sophisticated processing software, you can enhance the image to tell the story better and create an image that you love even more. Cropping out distractions, enhancing the colour, correcting the white balance and managing the exposure are all techniques that you can use to a greater or lesser extent - it's up to you. Make the image into what you want. Imperfections may enhance the story or distract the viewer - you can make the choice. You can change the image to black and white (I tend to always shoot colour film as I can easily change the scanned image to black and white should I wish), zoom in, change it to a square format, etc. Do not fall into the trap of thinking that you should accept the image as taken - it has already been processed in the camera - make it what you want. Once again, great photos do not have to have perfect focus and composition.

Twelve - Walk with others or alone. There is no right answer here, of course. You may prefer to walk alone, in a group of photographers or just a friend or loved one. Walking with others can help you get more from your Photo Walk, whether it be a shared experience, suggested shots, a willing subject or just a friendly chat before or after the shoot. And don't forget your pet too….. dogs can make great subjects on your Photo Walk. They see and hear things that you may miss walking alone. A dog's world is very different from ours. If you take your dog for a walk it starts as soon as you leave the house….. they do not wait to get somewhere, they just start…. a lesson for us all, maybe?

Thirteen - Visit more than once. The second visit to an area can often reveal more than the first Photo Walk. Look for photo opportunities from the changing seasons, light, buildings, farming and more. Whether the changes are punctuated by Christmas lights, plants in flower or the decay of an unkempt building revisiting a Photo Walk can help you see more and capture more. It's a good reason why capturing information about your Photo Walk in this Log Book can help you get great results.

Fourteen - Anticipate the weather and light conditions. It's good to anticipate the weather and light conditions that you can expect on your walk. You can then adjust the gear you carry - a compact weatherproof camera can help you enjoy the effects of the rain and reduce the challenges of trying to change lenses in the wet. Bright light may require a filter (polarizing or ND) or a lower ISO film. Don't forget your clothing and footwear too. Being too hot or too wet is not much fun when you want to focus on the Photo Walk. You will probably not want to carry your coat or arrive home with wet feet. Last on this subject, remember that the current weather does not always dictate what you will find on the walk. A dry sunny day does not mean that paths will be not wet and muddy from rain on previous days.

Fifteen - Plan your route. Planning your route may help you understand better what you are likely to see on your walk. Knowing what you may see can help you ensure you take the right gear and anticipate what the light conditions will be when you reach landmarks along your walk. You may want to check which direction to walk too (towards or away from the sun) and anticipate whether you will have long shadows, etc. Remember as you walk to make the most of everything around you by looking up, down and behind you, as well as in front. If you have some time when you are walking, you can always go back along your route to capture more shots.

Sixteen - Use Apps to help you get the most from your Photo Walk. There are lots of Apps that can help you with your Photo Walk from maps and navigation Apps (powered by GPS) to light meters and weather forecast Apps. You can also track your walk and use the track info in the future to log where you walked and where you took your images. If you want to add a location to your image and your camera does not have GPS - you can take an image with a smart phone and log your exact location - via the image's Exif data.

Seventeen - Look for angles and change heights. Sometimes when you are on a walk, you may find that you are taking all your photos at eye level in landscape or portrait. It's good to try different heights and angles - this can a be a little easier with some of the tilty / flippy screens available on some digital cameras. Remember as you walk to always look up and down as well as behind you for subject matter. Don't feel restricted to walking in one direction. You can always go back along your route to capture a new shot.

Eighteen - Stop, look, watch. Sometimes it's good to put your camera down and just watch the surrounding scenes. Observe what is happening the way the light falls, the routes that people take, the changing shadows, etc. You can then plan your next shots - or just enjoy the moment.

Nineteen - Review. Look through your images whilst on the walk (with a digital camera), when you process your images and perhaps before you visit the location on another occasions. Make reference to the notes in your Photo Walk Log. Decide what you like and what motivates you to be more creative.

Twenty - Share your images. Sharing images can be fun and informative - whether it be as a print or on social media. When you take a photo of someone and share it there are three people involved. You the photographer, the subject of the photograph and last but not least, the viewer. Should you choose to share your images we would love to see them via Instagram, just add #photowalkuk or via our Facebook Group facebook.com/groups/photowalkuk

HOW TO USE THE PHOTO WALK LOG BOOK

This Photo Walk Log Book is designed to help digital and film photographers record information when on a Photo Walk. It can create a permanent record so that the photographer can understand more about the images captured and perhaps input the information into Adobe Lightroom or similar in the future. The results should help you learn how best to use your cameras and to improve your photography skills and creativity.

You can complete the tables before, during and after your Photo Walk. Here are some tips for adding the right information.

Ref Number: Free field reference number. More specific to a Photo Walk than just location and references your walk information against shots. Could be added via Adobe Lightroom for future searches.

#photowalkuk: Add some hashtags for sharing walk images, for example specific Photo Walk hashtags such as #photowalkuksuffolk

Date and Time: Photo Walk Start information.

Objective/Theme: Examples could include environment specific (brutalist architecture) or camera specific (new 28mm lens)

Title/Town/Route: Great when you review images in the future.

Distance: You can add a note on the distance that you walked (There are lots of phone Apps that will record the distance walked)

Weather: Make reference to temperature, cloud cover, ground conditions, rain, etc. Add information about changes.

Light: Overall light conditions, shadow, sun position, etc. Use abbreviation such as OC for Overcast and BS for Bright Sun. This field could also be used to indicated whether a flash has been used or additional lighting such as LED lights.

Film Type ISO: Add the type/brand & speed of the film you are using e.g. Kodak Color 200. ISO stands for International Standards Organisation and it is a numerical value used by digital and film cameras to define the light sensitivity of the film. It will always be written on the film canister/box. You may also wish to add the expiry date of the film if it has already expired.

Exposure Modes - P, S, A, and M
P, S, A, M and C modes are known as exposure modes and give photographers a choice as to which elements of exposure—aperture or shutter speed—they wish to control.

> **P (Programmed Auto)** The camera automatically sets aperture and shutter speed for optimal exposure
> **S (Shutter-Priority Auto)** The photographer chooses the shutter speed and the camera automatically adjusts aperture for optimal exposure.
> **A (Aperture-Priority Auto)** The photographer chooses the aperture and the camera automatically adjusts shutter speed for optimal exposure.
> **M (Manual)** The photographer chooses both aperture and shutter speed.
> **C (Custom)** The photographer can pre-program the camera's settings, including ISO, focus mode, limits, and other special functions.

Equipment: When you view your photos later, you may want to check to see if the camera was handheld or attached to a tripod when looking at the sharpness for slow Shutter speeds. Add info on any filters used.

Camera: Add some details about your camera.

Lens mm: Add the focal length of the lens that is being used. This is most helpful for cameras that have interchangeable lenses like DSLRs. You can list the lenses used at the end of this Photo Walk Log and reference them e.g. 2Z.

Section Notes: With a digital camera you make take a large number of shots. The camera will record data as you shoot but these sections will be useful to include additional information about the Photo Walk. The sections maybe used for time, distance walked or particular environments or landmarks.

Image Ref: You may be able to extract an image reference from your camera at the start of each section to help you keep track of the shots you take on your Photo Walk. On an iPhone you can tap the ⓘ.

On a film camera, you can add an exposure number perhaps with total exposures such as 15/36 and on a digital camera, the image number.

Notes

Ref Number		#photowalkuk	
Date	Time	Objective/Theme	
Title/Town/Route			
			Distance
Weather			
Light			
Exposure Mode	P S A M C1 C2 C2 C3		Film Type & ISO
Equipment			
Camera		Lens	
Section 1 Notes			Image Ref
Section 2 Notes			Image Ref
Section 3 Notes			Image Ref
Section 4 Notes			Image Ref
Section 5 Notes			Image Ref
End Note			Image Ref

Ref Number		#photowalkuk	
Date	Time	Objective/Theme	
Title/Town/Route			
			Distance
Weather			
Light			
Exposure Mode	P S A M C1 C2 C2 C3		Film Type & ISO
Equipment			
Camera		Lens	

Section 1 Notes   Image Ref

Section 2 Notes   Image Ref

Section 3 Notes   Image Ref

Section 4 Notes   Image Ref

Section 5 Notes   Image Ref

End Note   Image Ref

Ref Number		#photowalkuk	
Date	Time	Objective/Theme	
Title/Town/Route			
		Distance	
Weather			
Light			
Exposure Mode	P S A M C1 C2 C2 C3	Film Type & ISO	
Equipment			
Camera		Lens	
Section 1 Notes		Image Ref	
Section 2 Notes		Image Ref	
Section 3 Notes		Image Ref	
Section 4 Notes		Image Ref	
Section 5 Notes		Image Ref	
End Note		Image Ref	

Ref Number		#photowalkuk	
Date	Time	Objective/Theme	
Title/Town/Route			
			Distance
Weather			
Light			
Exposure Mode	P S A M C1 C2 C2 C3		Film Type & ISO
Equipment			
Camera		Lens	
Section 1 Notes			Image Ref
Section 2 Notes			Image Ref
Section 3 Notes			Image Ref
Section 4 Notes			Image Ref
Section 5 Notes			Image Ref
End Note			Image Ref

Ref Number		#photowalkuk	
Date	Time	Objective/Theme	
Title/Town/Route			
		Distance	
Weather			
Light			
Exposure Mode	P S A M C1 C2 C2 C3	Film Type & ISO	
Equipment			
Camera		Lens	
Section 1 Notes		Image Ref	
Section 2 Notes		Image Ref	
Section 3 Notes		Image Ref	
Section 4 Notes		Image Ref	
Section 5 Notes		Image Ref	
End Note		Image Ref	

Ref Number		#photowalkuk	
Date	Time	Objective/Theme	
Title/Town/Route			
		Distance	
Weather			
Light			
Exposure Mode	P S A M C1 C2 C2 C3	Film Type & ISO	
Equipment			
Camera		Lens	
Section 1 Notes		Image Ref	
Section 2 Notes		Image Ref	
Section 3 Notes		Image Ref	
Section 4 Notes		Image Ref	
Section 5 Notes		Image Ref	
End Note		Image Ref	

Ref Number		#photowalkuk	
Date	Time	Objective/Theme	
Title/Town/Route			
		Distance	
Weather			
Light			
Exposure Mode	P S A M C1 C2 C2 C3	Film Type & ISO	
Equipment			
Camera		Lens	
Section 1 Notes		Image Ref	
Section 2 Notes		Image Ref	
Section 3 Notes		Image Ref	
Section 4 Notes		Image Ref	
Section 5 Notes		Image Ref	
End Note		Image Ref	

Ref Number		#photowalkuk	
Date	Time	Objective/Theme	
Title/Town/Route			
			Distance
Weather			
Light			
Exposure Mode	P S A M C1 C2 C2 C3		Film Type & ISO
Equipment			
Camera		Lens	
Section 1 Notes			Image Ref
Section 2 Notes			Image Ref
Section 3 Notes			Image Ref
Section 4 Notes			Image Ref
Section 5 Notes			Image Ref
End Note			Image Ref

Ref Number		#photowalkuk		
Date	Time	Objective/Theme		
Title/Town/Route				
			Distance	
Weather				
Light				
Exposure Mode	P S A M C1 C2 C2 C3		Film Type & ISO	
Equipment				
Camera		Lens		
Section 1 Notes			Image Ref	
Section 2 Notes			Image Ref	
Section 3 Notes			Image Ref	
Section 4 Notes			Image Ref	
Section 5 Notes			Image Ref	
End Note			Image Ref	

Ref Number		#photowalkuk	
Date	Time	Objective/Theme	
Title/Town/Route			
			Distance
Weather			
Light			
Exposure Mode	P S A M C1 C2 C2 C3	Film Type & ISO	
Equipment			
Camera		Lens	
Section 1 Notes			Image Ref
Section 2 Notes			Image Ref
Section 3 Notes			Image Ref
Section 4 Notes			Image Ref
Section 5 Notes			Image Ref
End Note			Image Ref

Ref Number		#photowalkuk	
Date	Time	Objective/Theme	
Title/Town/Route			
		Distance	
Weather			
Light			
Exposure Mode	P S A M C1 C2 C2 C3	Film Type & ISO	
Equipment			
Camera		Lens	
Section 1 Notes		Image Ref	
Section 2 Notes		Image Ref	
Section 3 Notes		Image Ref	
Section 4 Notes		Image Ref	
Section 5 Notes		Image Ref	
End Note		Image Ref	

Ref Number		#photowalkuk		
Date	Time	Objective/Theme		
Title/Town/Route				
			Distance	
Weather				
Light				
Exposure Mode	P S A M C1 C2 C2 C3		Film Type & ISO	
Equipment				
Camera		Lens		
Section 1 Notes			Image Ref	
Section 2 Notes			Image Ref	
Section 3 Notes			Image Ref	
Section 4 Notes			Image Ref	
Section 5 Notes			Image Ref	
End Note			Image Ref	

Ref Number		#photowalkuk		
Date	Time	Objective/Theme		
Title/Town/Route				
			Distance	
Weather				
Light				
Exposure Mode	P S A M C1 C2 C2 C3		Film Type & ISO	
Equipment				
Camera		Lens		
Section 1 Notes			Image Ref	
Section 2 Notes			Image Ref	
Section 3 Notes			Image Ref	
Section 4 Notes			Image Ref	
Section 5 Notes			Image Ref	
End Note			Image Ref	

Ref Number		#photowalkuk	
Date	Time	Objective/Theme	
Title/Town/Route			
			Distance
Weather			
Light			
Exposure Mode	P S A M C1 C2 C2 C3		Film Type & ISO
Equipment			
Camera		Lens	
Section 1 Notes			Image Ref
Section 2 Notes			Image Ref
Section 3 Notes			Image Ref
Section 4 Notes			Image Ref
Section 5 Notes			Image Ref
End Note			Image Ref

Ref Number		#photowalkuk	
Date	Time	Objective/Theme	
Title/Town/Route			
		Distance	
Weather			
Light			
Exposure Mode	P S A M C1 C2 C2 C3	Film Type & ISO	
Equipment			
Camera		Lens	
Section 1 Notes		Image Ref	
Section 2 Notes		Image Ref	
Section 3 Notes		Image Ref	
Section 4 Notes		Image Ref	
Section 5 Notes		Image Ref	
End Note		Image Ref	

Ref Number		#photowalkuk		
Date	Time	Objective/Theme		
Title/Town/Route				
			Distance	
Weather				
Light				
Exposure Mode	P S A M C1 C2 C2 C3		Film Type & ISO	
Equipment				
Camera		Lens		
Section 1 Notes			Image Ref	
Section 2 Notes			Image Ref	
Section 3 Notes			Image Ref	
Section 4 Notes			Image Ref	
Section 5 Notes			Image Ref	
End Note			Image Ref	

Ref Number		#photowalkuk	
Date	Time	Objective/Theme	
Title/Town/Route			
		Distance	
Weather			
Light			
Exposure Mode	P S A M C1 C2 C2 C3	Film Type & ISO	
Equipment			
Camera		Lens	
Section 1 Notes			Image Ref
Section 2 Notes			Image Ref
Section 3 Notes			Image Ref
Section 4 Notes			Image Ref
Section 5 Notes			Image Ref
End Note			Image Ref

Ref Number		#photowalkuk	
Date	Time	Objective/Theme	

Title/Town/Route			
		Distance	

Weather		

Light		

Exposure Mode	P S A M C1 C2 C2 C3	Film Type & ISO

Equipment	

Camera		Lens	

Section 1 Notes			Image Ref

Section 2 Notes			Image Ref

Section 3 Notes			Image Ref

Section 4 Notes			Image Ref

Section 5 Notes			Image Ref

End Note			Image Ref

Ref Number		#photowalkuk		
Date	Time	Objective/Theme		
Title/Town/Route				
			Distance	
Weather				
Light				
Exposure Mode	P S A M C1 C2 C2 C3		Film Type & ISO	
Equipment				
Camera		Lens		
Section 1 Notes			Image Ref	
Section 2 Notes			Image Ref	
Section 3 Notes			Image Ref	
Section 4 Notes			Image Ref	
Section 5 Notes			Image Ref	
End Note			Image Ref	

Ref Number		#photowalkuk	
Date	Time	Objective/Theme	
Title/Town/Route			
		Distance	
Weather			
Light			
Exposure Mode	P S A M C1 C2 C2 C3	Film Type & ISO	
Equipment			
Camera		Lens	

Section 1 Notes			Image Ref

Section 2 Notes			Image Ref

Section 3 Notes			Image Ref

Section 4 Notes			Image Ref

Section 5 Notes			Image Ref

| End Note | | | Image Ref |

Ref Number		#photowalkuk	
Date	Time	Objective/Theme	
Title/Town/Route			
		Distance	
Weather			
Light			
Exposure Mode	P S A M C1 C2 C2 C3	Film Type & ISO	
Equipment			
Camera		Lens	
Section 1 Notes			Image Ref
Section 2 Notes			Image Ref
Section 3 Notes			Image Ref
Section 4 Notes			Image Ref
Section 5 Notes			Image Ref
End Note			Image Ref

Ref Number		#photowalkuk	
Date	Time	Objective/Theme	
Title/Town/Route			
			Distance
Weather			
Light			
Exposure Mode	P S A M C1 C2 C2 C3		Film Type & ISO
Equipment			
Camera		Lens	

Section 1 Notes			Image Ref

Section 2 Notes			Image Ref

Section 3 Notes			Image Ref

Section 4 Notes			Image Ref

Section 5 Notes			Image Ref

End Note			Image Ref

Ref Number		#photowalkuk	
Date	Time	Objective/Theme	
Title/Town/Route			
		Distance	
Weather			
Light			
Exposure Mode	P S A M C1 C2 C2 C3	Film Type & ISO	
Equipment			
Camera		Lens	
Section 1 Notes		Image Ref	
Section 2 Notes		Image Ref	
Section 3 Notes		Image Ref	
Section 4 Notes		Image Ref	
Section 5 Notes		Image Ref	
End Note		Image Ref	

Ref Number		#photowalkuk	
Date	Time	Objective/Theme	
Title/Town/Route			
		Distance	
Weather			
Light			
Exposure Mode	P S A M C1 C2 C2 C3	Film Type & ISO	
Equipment			
Camera		Lens	

Section 1 Notes		Image Ref	

Section 2 Notes		Image Ref	

Section 3 Notes		Image Ref	

Section 4 Notes		Image Ref	

Section 5 Notes		Image Ref	

End Note		Image Ref	

Ref Number		#photowalkuk	
Date	Time	Objective/Theme	
Title/Town/Route			
		Distance	
Weather			
Light			
Exposure Mode	P S A M C1 C2 C2 C3	Film Type & ISO	
Equipment			
Camera		Lens	
Section 1 Notes		Image Ref	
Section 2 Notes		Image Ref	
Section 3 Notes		Image Ref	
Section 4 Notes		Image Ref	
Section 5 Notes		Image Ref	
End Note		Image Ref	

Ref Number		#photowalkuk	
Date	Time	Objective/Theme	
Title/Town/Route			
		Distance	
Weather			
Light			
Exposure Mode	P S A M C1 C2 C2 C3	Film Type & ISO	
Equipment			
Camera		Lens	
Section 1 Notes			Image Ref
Section 2 Notes			Image Ref
Section 3 Notes			Image Ref
Section 4 Notes			Image Ref
Section 5 Notes			Image Ref
End Note			Image Ref

Ref Number		#photowalkuk	
Date	Time	Objective/Theme	
Title/Town/Route			
		Distance	
Weather			
Light			
Exposure Mode	P S A M C1 C2 C2 C3	Film Type & ISO	
Equipment			
Camera		Lens	
Section 1 Notes			Image Ref
Section 2 Notes			Image Ref
Section 3 Notes			Image Ref
Section 4 Notes			Image Ref
Section 5 Notes			Image Ref
End Note			Image Ref

Ref Number		#photowalkuk		
Date	Time	Objective/Theme		
Title/Town/Route				
			Distance	
Weather				
Light				
Exposure Mode	P S A M C1 C2 C2 C3		Film Type & ISO	
Equipment				
Camera		Lens		
Section 1 Notes			Image Ref	
Section 2 Notes			Image Ref	
Section 3 Notes			Image Ref	
Section 4 Notes			Image Ref	
Section 5 Notes			Image Ref	
End Note			Image Ref	

Ref Number		#photowalkuk		
Date	Time	Objective/Theme		
Title/Town/Route				
			Distance	
Weather				
Light				
Exposure Mode	P S A M C1 C2 C2 C3		Film Type & ISO	
Equipment				
Camera		Lens		
Section 1 Notes			Image Ref	
Section 2 Notes			Image Ref	
Section 3 Notes			Image Ref	
Section 4 Notes			Image Ref	
Section 5 Notes			Image Ref	
End Note			Image Ref	

Ref Number		#photowalkuk		
Date	Time	Objective/Theme		
Title/Town/Route				
			Distance	
Weather				
Light				
Exposure Mode	P S A M C1 C2 C2 C3		Film Type & ISO	
Equipment				
Camera		Lens		
Section 1 Notes			Image Ref	
Section 2 Notes			Image Ref	
Section 3 Notes			Image Ref	
Section 4 Notes			Image Ref	
Section 5 Notes			Image Ref	
End Note			Image Ref	

Ref Number		#photowalkuk		
Date	Time	Objective/Theme		
Title/Town/Route				
			Distance	
Weather				
Light				
Exposure Mode	P S A M C1 C2 C2 C3		Film Type & ISO	
Equipment				
Camera		Lens		
Section 1 Notes			Image Ref	
Section 2 Notes			Image Ref	
Section 3 Notes			Image Ref	
Section 4 Notes			Image Ref	
Section 5 Notes			Image Ref	
End Note			Image Ref	

Ref Number		#photowalkuk	
Date	Time	Objective/Theme	
Title/Town/Route			
			Distance
Weather			
Light			
Exposure Mode	P S A M C1 C2 C2 C3		Film Type & ISO
Equipment			
Camera		Lens	
Section 1 Notes			Image Ref
Section 2 Notes			Image Ref
Section 3 Notes			Image Ref
Section 4 Notes			Image Ref
Section 5 Notes			Image Ref
End Note			Image Ref

APPENDICES

THE LAW AND PHOTOGRAPHY - UK

Taking photographs is fun and rewarding but is of course best to keep within the law. The Yashica 35 range is often considered to be a great for street photography. This appendix is just a high-level summary regarding some elements of the law and taking photographs in the UK. The photographer is always best to seek permission to take a photograph either from the subject in the case of a person or owner in the case of a property.

On the whole, UK law does not prevent photography in public places. The UK has relatively liberal laws regarding photography compared with many countries. Although there are some exceptions, the key principle is that you can photograph people and buildings without needing permission, providing you are in a public place.

PRIVATE PROPERTY

The definition of private property is wide and includes areas that might appear to be publicly owned in the UK like shopping centres, museums and sports centres. Owners of property do not normally have the right to prevent someone from taking photographs of their property from a public place such as a public highway, (but there are expectations). There is also no general restriction on taking photographs while on private property, provided the photographer has permission to be on the property. However, the property owner has the right to impose whatever conditions they wish on entry to the property, including a restriction on photography. Examples include art galleries, museums and stately homes, concert venues and some shopping centres.

A person who enters onto private property without permission commits a trespass, as does anyone who 'interferes' with the property. Interference could be something as minor as climbing on the landowners wall to take a photograph over the wall or resting a camera on a fence. If a person has permission to enter property on the condition that he does not take photographs, but ignores the condition, they become a trespasser as soon as a photo is taken. Even where property is open to entry by the public in general, as in the case of most business premises, the owner or occupier has the right to demand that a photographer ceases taking photographs and the right to demand that they leave the premises. Trespass law is complicated and out of scope of this book so it is best to always ask for permission before taking photographs.

It is a criminal offence to trespass on some types of property, including railways, airports, military bases. Anyone who enters onto these kinds of premises without permission is liable to be arrested. There are often very clear warning. signs.

RESTRICTIONS ON PHOTOGRAPHY IN CERTAIN PUBLIC PLACES.

With the ubiquitous use of phones with cameras it is often thought that restrictions have all been relaxed and forgotten in public places. But there is a prohibition on taking photographs in areas such as Trafalgar Square, Parliament Square and the Royal Parks in London for photographs taken in connection with any business, profession or employment without permission.

TAKING PHOTOGRAPHS OF PEOPLE

Lots has been written about taking photographs of people and street photography rights. The first thing to say is that it is illegal to harass another person and taking photographs could be considered as harassment. This is not to say that someone could claim they were being harassed just because they were being photographed when they did not want to be. Harassment is essentially behaviour that causes another person alarm or distress and it refers to a course of conduct (at least two occasions), not a single incident. If a photographer stalks a subject in order to get a photograph of them, or repeatedly thrusts a camera in someone's face, this might be harassment.

The use of a long lens to take a photo of someone in a private place, such as their home, without their consent, is an invasion of privacy even though the photo is taken from a public place.

For images of people in public places, the key seems to be whether the place is one where a person would have a reasonable expectation of privacy and the courts have greatly extended the areas where this might be the case. A court has held that the right of privacy of a child might be infringed by the taking and publishing of a photograph of them with his parents in a public street. The general advice is to get consent, and preferably written consent, wherever possible. Failure to obtain a signed model release will certainly impair the commercial use of an image, because many photo libraries, stock agencies and the like will not accept an image of a recognisable person without a release (there than for an editorial licence under certain circumstances).
Photographs of people may also be subject to the Data Protection Act, which controls the "processing" of "personal data", that is, data relating to an individual and from which the individual can be identified. The Act contains an exception for processing undertaken with a view to publication of any

journalistic, literary or artistic material, if certain criteria are met.

PHOTOGRAPHS OF CHILDREN

The law relating to harassment, invasion of privacy and data protection
applies in the same way to children as to adults, but a child does not have the
legal capacity to consent and a parent or guardian must consent on his behalf.
A child under 16 cannot be used as a paid model unless a licence is obtained
from the local authority. It is not illegal as such to photograph children in a
public place, however in some circumstances it will almost certainly draw the
attention of the police and may result in the photographer being investigated.

Obstruction and Public Order - It is a criminal offence to obstruct free passage
on the highway and this includes footways and cycle paths and roads.
Whether a photographer will be treated as causing an obstruction depends on
the reasonableness of his behaviour. Setting up a tripod in a busy street is
obviously likely to cause an obstruction. The police will usually initially ask
the photographer to move along rather than arrest him, unless his behaviour is
persistent.

Another obstruction offence is that of obstructing a police officer in the
execution of his duty. This basically means doing anything that makes it more
difficult for the police to carry out their duties effectively. Getting in the way of
the police while trying to photograph an incident, for example, would be
obstructing them.

Photographers who are shooting incidents such as riots and illegal
demonstrations should take care that the police don't confuse them with the
participants. The best advice is to stay calm, do not argue and move further
from the scene if requested to do so by the police. Refusal might lead to an
arrest for obstruction.

National Security - In recent years, sensitivity over issues of security and
prevention of terrorism has been very high. This has led to photographers
being confronted by police when taking photographs of subjects that
previously would not have been thought of as particularly sensitive.

Two areas of the law might come into play to restrict the right to take
photographs of certain places. It an offence to take or possess a photograph
containing information likely to be useful to a person committing or preparing
an act of terrorism (s.58) And since February 2009, it is an offence to elicit or
attempt to elicit information about anyone who is or who has been a member
of the armed force, the police or the intelligence services, where this is of a
kind likely to be useful to a person committing or preparing an act of terrorism

(s.58A). Some police officers appear to take a fairly broad view of "information likely to be useful", but courts have been rather more restrictive in their interpretation of s.58. It is always in a photographer's best interests to cooperate with the police if they approach when photos are being taken in an area that might be regarded as sensitive.

COURT PROCEEDINGS

It is a criminal offence to take a photograph in a law court, and an additional offence to publish any photo taken in a court. This restriction extends beyond the courtroom itself.

WILDLIFE

Many wild animals, including insects, and birds are protected by the Wildlife and Countryside Act There is no restriction on taking photographs of any animal or bird, but the Act makes it an offence to "disturb" some species when they at or near their nesting places or places of shelter. This includes disturbing them by taking photographs of them.

COPYRIGHT AND TRADEMARKS

It will sometimes be an infringement of copyright to take a photograph of a work that is protected by copyright. Copyright is infringed by making a copy of all or a substantial part of a copyright work, without the consent of the copyright owner. It would therefore be an infringement of copyright to take a photograph of a copyright protected artwork, or a photograph of a photograph.

THE LAW - OUTSIDE OF THE UK

Laws in other countries differ from the UK. In the USA, for example, local, state, and national laws govern still and motion photography. Laws therefore vary between jurisdictions, and what is not illegal in one place may be illegal in another.

See resource page:

rwjemmett.com/photowalklog

LOG BOOK NOTES

This Log Book was designed and published by RW Jemmett.

Find out more about this Log Book

rwjemmett.com/photowalklog

This Log Book belongs to.

Name:

Contact:

Log Book Number:

Dates: From: To:

Cameras Used:
1
2
3
4
5

Lenses Used:
1
2
3
4
5
6
7

Custom Settings:
C1
C2
C3
C4

EQUIPMENT CHECK

- Camera(s)
- Batteries
- SD Cards
- Filters
- Tripod
- Lens cloth
- USB cable
- Lenses
- Camera case
- Photo Walk Log Book
- Pencil/pen

Notes

Printed in Dunstable, United Kingdom